CASSELL'S POCKET LIBRARY

❖ ❖ ❖

JOAN OF ARC

JOAN OF ARC

by

HILAIRE BELLOC

CASSELL & COMPANY LTD

LONDON, TORONTO, MELBOURNE, SYDNEY

First Published   May,   1929
Second Impression October,   1929
Pocket Edition   September, 1930

Printed in Great Britain

To
MY DAUGHTER
ELIZABETH

❖ ❖ ❖

CONTENTS

I

I

FIVE HUNDRED years ago, and more, there was in France an old mad King whose wife was a German harlot, mocking him. All in his realm was distracted; for when kingship is weak the powerful oppress and destroy. And among the miseries of the time was this : that the kingdom was riven by rivals.

For King John of the family of Valois, the grandfather of the old mad King (the same who had fought against the King of England at Crecy and had been made Prisoner at Poitiers), had been well defended in battle by a young son of his called Philip, and to reward him he called him " Philip the Bold " and gave him the great Province of Burgundy, to the

east, to govern, making him Duke of Burgundy, him and his sons after him. But this he was to hold in fealty of the King his father, and later of the Kings his successors ; which he did.

But when King John was long dead, and his grandsons were Duke of Burgundy and King of France, the new Duke of Burgundy was galled by his subjection to his cousin the King of France : for he was powerful in his own country and secretly desired to break faith and hold it alone and free. So when it was seen that his cousin the King of France would remain of feeble mind, Burgundy took the right to rule in his name. But the mad King's own brother (who was called Duke of Orleans) challenged, and a bitter feud arose between them as to which should govern in the name of the mad King ; and the people of France and the priests and bishops and nobles, and the lawyers and learned doctors of the universities, made

two parties, some for Burgundy and some for Orleans, so they were like two nations; until, in an evil day, Burgundy had Orleans murdered.

Then, indeed, it was War. And as the young Duke of Orleans, the son of the murdered man, had married the daughter of a strong Lord of the South, called Armagnac, those of his party were called "The Armagnacs" and those of Burgundy were called "The Burgundians," in the French "Bourgignon"; and they fought against one another which should hold Paris, the head city of the realm, and rule the King; and they laid the realm waste between them with foul massacres and burnings.

Now the Kings of England in those days were also born of great French Princes being of the family of Plantagenet from Anjou, and they had long claimed to be rightful Kings of France through a Princess of France, heiress

of that country (whose tongue also they spoke,
as did their nobles), and called themselves of
better right than the family of Valois. So,
seeing how distraught and weakened were the
Valois by this deadly quarrel of Armagnac
and Bourgignon, Valois Orleans against Valois
Burgundy, the King of England, Henry Plantagenet, fifth of that name, came into France
with an army small, but very good. He over-
threw the great host of the Armagnacs at
Agincourt and took prisoner the young Duke
of Orleans himself (the Burgundians refusing
aid), and went on to take the castles and walled
towns of the north one after another, even
great Rouen after a dreadful siege ; and, even
as he was so conquering, the Armagnacs,
remembering the murder of the elder Duke of
Orleans, murdered the Duke of Burgundy in
their turn. His young son, a mighty soldier,
was filled with vengeance and joined the

English King; saying also, within himself:
"So shall I be more free when the King of
France is dead."

But this new Duke of Burgundy, Philip by
name, was of the strongest spirit among the
great of his day, and had a face hard and eager
as though carven of dark wood, and above his
eyes were thick black brows with ends that
rose upwards, so that, when he was in his angers,
men said they seemed like horns.

That German harlot the Queen of France
had given aid first to one side and then to the
other, and now that Burgundy was master—
for he held Paris and with him was the
Plantagenet—she declared for him (whom she
had long supported) and favoured his plan;
which was this: that Henry should marry her
daughter and be Regent of France abetting
Burgundy's power, and that the child of Henry
and her daughter should be King of France

when the mad King should die. For she said that this daughter of hers was the rightful heir, being the mad King's true daughter. And although she had a son also living, called Charles (a very young man whom the Armagnacs protected and to whom of plain right should fall the Kingdom), this son, she said, was no true heir.

For she was so shameless that she called him Bastard, saying that the poor mad King was not his father; and she was such a wanton that many believed her. For they said: "Would his own mother call him Bastard if he were not so?"

But she lied, as she ever did; for that very young man was indeed the mad King's son and the true Heir to France, so that he was called the Dauphin, which was the title now borne by the eldest prince of the Blood Royal. He and his had no strength to stand against their

enemies, and he had fled southward beyond Loire, when, soon after, in the year of Our Lord fourteen hundred and twenty-two, Henry Plantagenet King of England died, leaving a baby boy nine months old, the son of himself and that French Princess by their marriage, whom they called Henry, sixth of that name. And two months later the old mad King died too. The baby boy Henry should have been crowned at Rheims if indeed Burgundy would make him King of France, for that was the rightful place of Crowning and Anointing for the Kings of France, and was in Burgundian power. But the dead King Henry's brother, Duke of Bedford, who had been left Regent, dared not take so young a child many leagues through country where war-bands roved, and he put off to some later time the solemnity of Rheims which alone made a King of France very King in his people's eyes.

B

Yet all things opposed the Dauphin, Charles of Valois; for strong Burgundy held all the east and Bedford all the north, and they were allied, with Paris in their hold and favouring them. His poor forces were discouraged, his captains blundered, he was but nineteen, and weak of blood with feeble legs beneath him and a soul too timid, his counsellors foolish or false and his moneys failing. Of his own people, daily more abandoned him, and the Church, the ancient prop of his royal house, was divided.

For two Popes and even three had but lately claimed one against the other, bringing the Vicarship of Christ to mockery; and the Churchmen had made a great Council which called itself the Church and gave out its power to make and unmake the Lordship of Christian men and to be supreme even over the Chair of Peter, and soon was to be another Council, with

Burgundy and the English for the Council, and the Dauphin Charles for the Pope : all was in confusion. Therefore many Bishops and great Abbots and the University of Paris, to whose voice all men attended, favoured his foes.

Allies he had none, save the Scottish people, the unceasing enemies of England. These indeed had sent him very good soldiers, but few, and at Verneuil, when he desperately tried his chance in battle, his battalions were scattered. His men still fought, had the better of a skirmish, relieved a stronghold ; but the darkness grew. Town upon town and castle upon castle declared for the enemy. St. Denis, the shrine of the Kings and their sacred Oriflamme, was in his foeman's hands, and the myriads of Paris —or their chiefs—were against him. He had no hope but by offers to wean his cousin Philip of Burgundy from Bedford and the Plantagenet

child ; a tangled intrigue without issue, for no one about him could fathom Burgundy, his deep and subtle mind.

The common people of the countrysides had in them indeed a memory of the Crown and of the Lilies, the heart of Christendom from the days of their fathers' fathers, from the days when the Faith first grew strong in their hearts. But no man moved.

So things stood when, the old mad King being now dead these six years gone, and the Dauphin twenty-five years old, Bedford moved for the final throw. He would take Orleans upon the Loire, the fortress which forbade the passage of the river ; and after he had taken Orleans he would cross the stream and hold the south, and so at last all France. In the summer he raised forces in England with many guns great and small. In the autumn he drew his lines round Orleans. It was October in the

year of Our Lord fourteen hundred and twenty-eight.

Shut in his closet, alone, the Dauphin despaired. A doubt took him whether such misfortunes were not proof that the tale was true, and he none of the King's blood. He prayed there, apart, a strong particular prayer, well remembered, deeply graven into his heart. In this prayer he prayed that if indeed he were not of the Blood Royal but a Bastard born as his base mother had proclaimed, then let God remove from his heart the desire for sovereignty. But at least not to let him be killed or captured, but escape to safeguard in the Court of Castille or of Scotland, friends from of old with the Lilies. And he besought God, if indeed he were Dauphin of the Great Line, to grant him a sign. But how could a sign be given ? So he . prayed; and he told no man living of that prayer.

While these evils were happening, James d'Arc and his wife Isabel of Domrémy in the Marches of Lorraine, had born to them on the Epiphany, in the year of Our Lord fourteen hundred and twelve, a girl child whom they called Joan on the day when she was baptized into the Church of God.

She grew up tall and sturdy, strong of body and clear of mind, and vigorous at her tasks of spinning and all housework; she would tend sheep and she would plough upon their half-hundred acres, for her father was a yeoman. Also she was famous at her needle. As a child she played round the Fairies' beech tree in the place, hanging garlands, singing and dancing there, she and her three brothers and her little sister Catherine and the other children of the hamlet; and at home her mother taught her the Hail Mary and the Our Father and the Creed. It was in a pleasant valley with long

hills on either side and woods upon them, and the young river Meuse flowed by.

One summer morning when she was thirteen years of age and some months more, she went into the meadows to gather flowers with her companions and they ran races together, till she heard a lad saying: "Your mother needs you." Joan therefore went back quickly to the house, for she was kept subject. But her mother wondered and said she had not summoned her; so Joan went out again from the door into the garden-close and stood there a moment looking westward towards the near hills. It was noon.

As she so stood a dazzling light shone by her at her right hand, supplanting the day, and she was overcome with terror; till, from the midst of the glory, came a Voice which spoke of the Faith and its observance, and at last gave order that she should seek the uncrowned King of France, dispossessed by his foes, and rescue

him and crown him at Rheims. At the third summons she saw St. Michael in his splendour and about him the Soldiery of Heaven.

She was so young, and trembling, that she told no one (save later, secretly, the Priest), but she turned to a new piety as she grew into womanhood, cherishing the poor, and at her prayers continually till her devotion seemed ridiculous to those about her. And she had vowed her virginity to God "so long as it should Him please," but on this also she held her peace.

The summer passed and the winter; her summoning Heralds from beatitude would not let her be, but urged her still. There came Saint Catherine and Saint Margaret, who called each other by their names, and who were fragrant, speaking in low and lovely voices and still proclaiming her, and week after week, every two days or three, she lived in this companion-

ship, consecrated, hesitant, impelled. There was the world about her, but there were also These : " I saw them with the eyes of my body, as plainly as I see you now ; and when they went away, I would cry. For I wanted them to take me with them,"—to that Paradise. Yet she still withstood them and was silent. Not till the third year did she yield and speak.

It was the week of the Ascension, in that same spring when Bedford was sending message to raise those new forces in England, the year fourteen hundred and twenty-eight, the month of May, and Joan not yet seventeen years old.

Down the valley a dozen miles from Domrémy stood the little walled town of Vaucouleurs, which Robert de Baudricourt (a rough man of common mind, a noble, and a good soldier, wealthy, downright), held for the true King. Those walls alone were held in all that countryside. For all Champagne, on the edge

of which lay Domrémy, was the enemy's, and so were the strongholds all round about, though the fields lay open.

An hour's walk and less from Vaucouleurs, in Little Burey, lived one Lassois, who had for wife Joan's cousin : but he was far older than she. Now Joan had mind to visit Vaucouleurs for a set purpose and she found a plea. Lassois's wife, her cousin, was to have a child, and Joan asked him whether she could not be of service about the house—so could she go off unhindered. For she feared her father on account of a dream of his, which was this : two years before, or nearly two years, he had dreamt that he saw his daughter riding off with armed men, and when he woke the dream still troubled him. He misread it to mean that she was destined to go off loosely following some band and he said : " If she did thus I would drown her " ; and to his sons : " If I do not drown her for it with

my own hands, you must drown her." The
dream and its false reading were fading from his
mind, but she still feared.

In Lassois's house did she first speak and said:
"Have you not heard how France, laid waste
by a woman, shall be restored by a Maid?"
And such a prophecy indeed had run, older
than she; for a woman in the south had uttered
it long before, and during the grievous ruin that
the Queen had made it spread widely: and
there were older, darker sayings.

Next, Joan bade Lassois take her to the
Governor's hall in Vaucouleurs, and there
Baudricourt saw her, and with him a man in
his thirties, one Poulengy, who later bore
witness to her. She came dressed in the rough
serge of dark red which the women wore who
worked in the fields, and gave the Governor her
message—which was in his ears pure folly. But
she added this, which in time should give him

pause : " Send word to the Dauphin, that he
ward him well and beware of giving battle.
By Mid-Lent Our Lord will send him aid."

His answer was to bid the man take her back
to her father. He sent her away for a rustic
trickster or a half-wit of the furrows.

She had broken silence, but she was still
chary of speech. It was five weeks later, on
the eve of St. John, that she said to a boy of
the village how that a girl from that valley
would crown the King at Rheims " within the
year."

The story went the rounds. There passed
through the village a young man on his travels
in that season, and he also heard it, and bore
testimony to it after thirty years.

During that summer it grew. In July the
enemy had sent a raiding party against the
valley and to take Vaucouleurs. It failed—but
they of Domrémy took refuge in Neufchâteau,

southwards, a couple of hours up the valley, and there, in the inn where she and her people stayed, the thing was known. Some say that it was for this cause that her father, no longer believing evil of her desire to ride, but wishing to keep her at home, promised her in marriage. We do not know. But she was claimed as affianced, and cleared herself in the Bishop's court at Toul, a long day's ride away. If others had promised her, she had not consented. She had vowed herself to God.

In the late summer came rumours of movement far away to the north and the west. The levies from England were on the march from the Channel. In October—at its close—came the news of the final throw. The Siege of Orleans had begun. The story of its fortunes came confused to that remote place, but a peasantry is full of news from drovers and market-men, and in those days all heard and

debated the things of the Commonwealth. Far more and quite apart was the insistence of the Voices and of them that conversed with her : " Go ! Go ! When you find the King at Chinon you shall have the Sign ! " The command controlled her, and, by the end of the year, go she must. She longed " as a woman to be delivered."

She bade no farewells to father or to mother or to the young companions, saving that as she passed she called to little Hauviette her friend, but for the second time she set her face north-ward for Vaucouleurs. Nor did she ever again see the smoke rising from her own roof, Domrémy and the woods of home.

Six weeks (at Burey first with the Lassois, later in the town at the house of one Leroyer) she was held, waiting. Baudricourt would not move. The old Duke of Lorraine, curious to see wonders, sent for her to Nancy, whither

she came and saw him, had from him a sorry
horse to ride back on, no other succour. But
in that chafing of delay she found her first
companion in faith. It was a young man-at-
arms, called "of Metz" and from his land
"John of Nouillonpont," who asked her what
her call was and whether the King must fall.
To whom she answered: "I am come to a
King's town to crave of Robert de Baudricourt
that he send me to my King. He contemns me
and heeds not what I say. Yet must I be with
my King by Mid-Lent though I walk and wear
my legs to the knees, since none can succour
him—nor Scots King's daughter, nor Dukes
nor Kings. Go I must, for my Lord wills
it so."

"And who is your Lord?"

"God is my Lord," she said.

Then this young man, John of Nouillonpont,
ten years older than she, swore between her

hands that he would serve her, saying : " God aiding, I will lead you to the King."

And she answered : " Better to-day than to-morrow, better to-morrow than later yet."

Then for the last time she would speak with Baudricourt. But now she brought a Sign.

It was Saturday the 12th of February. She told him that he did grievously ill to keep her back ; for on that very day the armies of his Prince had suffered sheer rout before Orleans and there was high peril. Now in a week and a little more there came riding into Vaucouleurs a King's messenger, Colet of Vienne, who had pressed hard day upon day and who brought news, weary on a weary steed. There had been rout before Orleans and a field lost at Rouvray, to the peril of the despairing cause ; for the English, bringing provisions to their siege-army,

had found their way barred by the Dauphin's men and their Scots allies, but had overthrown them utterly: as for the day, why it had fallen on the Saturday, the 12th, just gone. On hearing this the Governor was halted and marvelled, remembering what Joan had said even while that far fight was on. So he fetched a priest and, breaking into Leroyer's house, bade him exorcise. The Priest, in stole and with book, cried to That which filled her: "If thou art of Evil depart, but if of Good come forward," and she came forward on her knees. But she vowed that it was ill done, for this Priest had confessed and absolved her, and knew that she was of God.

Then Baudricourt could no longer deny. Poulengy and Nouillonpont had a horse (of no great worth) bought for her, and Baudricourt suffered her to put on a man's dress and

C

permitted her escort, so that by Tuesday the
22nd she was ready, and on the morrow she rode
out westward at evening by the French Gate
with her companions, who were that same King's
messenger that had come so lately and must now
return, and Poulengy and Nouillonpont, each
with his serving man. So there were seven
companions riding out together to their
King.

But she would not call him King but only
Dauphin, for he was not crowned till she should
crown him. Those who looked on her in the
last of the winter light as she rode westward
(for they would travel by dark for fear of
wandering bands) saw her astride in her man's
garb as having to consort with men and to bear
arms; a black doublet and cap, grey tunic and
trunk-hose, and gaitered to the knees, and
spurred.

They rode by devious ways and much by

night for fear of those armed bands which laid waste the countrysides (and often they slept in the open, for they feared alarms) to the monastery of St. Urban over the hills, to the tiles of Auxerre, to Gien ; ten, fifteen, leagues at a time, and all the while in the enemy's land and hearing mass where they could. At last, at Gien, they came to the Loire river, beyond which was the land the Dauphin still held, and they were in safety. On the tenth day they were at that famous shrine of St. Catharine of Fierbois, and Chinon and the court but three hours ahead. There did she hear her three masses, and thence did she send and have written for her (she did not commonly write, save her name) a letter to her King, wherein she told him she should know him among all others. On the morrow they came by morning down the road to the river-bank and saw before them the hill and the high hall-roof and the

long walls of Chinon Castle and the town below.

They had come two hundred miles and fifty and more ; and it was Sunday, the sixth day of March, in this year of Our Lord fourteen hundred and twenty-nine.

II

II

JOAN AND her companions, having come into Chinon, dined there at an inn of good repute, and would have gone up in the afternoon to the Castle on the height to ask audience of Charles the true King. But because he was consulting on her coming she was not then received, nor the next day. But on the Tuesday, after the sun had set, she got word and they went up the steep to the Castle gate.

On that way there passed them a soldier on horseback who, because the coming of the Maid was known and quarrelled on in the guard-room (some for, some against), or because she and her companions left but a narrow pass at

the drawbridge, swore loudly in the dusk at
Joan : who answered gravely :

" In the name of God, do you swear ? And
you so near your death ? "

And in one hour, night having fallen and it
being the dark of the moon, he missed his way
and came into the water and was drowned.

But Joan and her companions went up into
the Castle, and she was taken through the stone
passage to the great hall which stands by the
southern wall overlooking the town, and so
came suddenly into the great hall, still dressed
in her man's clothes in grey hose and tunic
but with the black jacket over, tall, and her
dark hair cut round at the neck as a man's
would be.

That high room was filled very full with all
the people of the court, all splendid each in the
robes of his order and the jewels and gold of
their estates, and the colours of their silks and

velvets ; and there was light from fifty cressets
hanging from the walls. In that hall were
Regnault of Chartres, Archbishop of Rheims
and Primate of the Realm, and that huge-
bellied man La Trémoille, very rich, intriguing,
who had most power with the hesitating King,
and Gaucourt, who speaks of that day, and a
crowd besides ; three hundred in all, full of talk
and moving till she came. But, half a week
away lay Orleans besieged, with the English
works about it ; even that day had reinforcement for them come in from the north, and
their cannon was speaking. There did she long
to be.

It was Louis de Bourbon, Count of Vendôme,
of the Blood Royal (for he also came from St.
Louis through his fathers), who led Joan in,
nor was she abashed nor forward, but simple
and straight in her carriage. But they who
had heard how she had said that she would know

the King by divine power, said to her, pointing as she passed : "Look! There is the King!" and showed her another ; or again : "Look! He is there!" For the King, to try her, had taken care to put on no mark of rank or to stand apart or receive deference, but was dressed as any other might be and mixed in with the crowd.

But she went straight up to him, as to a mark, without halt or turning, and knelt before him, and said, looking up into his face :

"God give you long life, noble King."

Charles said to her : "I am not the King."

She answered : "In God's name, Sir, you are the King, and no other! Give me troops wherewith to succour Orleans and to guard you to Rheims to be anointed and crowned. For it is the Will of God."

Then did Charles take her apart somewhat and talk to her privately, seeing that she had

known him. But what they said together we are not told. Yet, whether it were then or a little later, this we know : that the Sign whereby the King should know she was from God was given, and his mind was changed by it. For what Joan did was this :

She told him of the time when he, Charles of Valois, Dauphin of France and true King, of the Blood Royal, had, in a memorable day, withdrawn from all other men and prayed a special prayer in his oratory quite alone, doubting his own lineage and his right. If indeed he were not of the Blood Royal but a Bastard born as his base mother had proclaimed, then let God remove from his heart the desire for sovereignty. But at least let him not be killed or captured, but escape to safeguard in the court of Castille or of Scotland, friends from of old with the Lilies.

Now this was known to none but to himself

who had so prayed, and to God, for no whisper
of such doubts in his heart could be heard from
him for very shame. Yet Joan told him of
that prayer, having had knowledge of it from
her Kinsmen of Paradise.

Such was the Sign, and it was of power.

. . . . .

There stood upon the curtain-wall of Chinon
Castle a tower called " The Tower of Coudray,"
where lodged an officer of the court, one
William Bellier and his wife. There, and with
them, was Joan lodged and given a household,
as one of consequence, with a little page
fourteen years old, called Louis de Coutes, who
long years after remembered her prayers and
her fervour, and who would marvel at the great
men coming in and out to speak with her. Later
also she had a knight for steward and fighting
comrade, a man of birth, famous in the fighting,
John of Aulon, and a chaplain, one John

Pasquerel, an Augustinian who was her confessor ; but she confessed also to others and had no one director in the things of the soul. For her mind would not follow another's mind save those of her Visitors, the Holy Ones who were so beautiful and brought with them the airs of Heaven.

There was at court in those days a high young noble, also of the Blood Royal, fair, very brave and perpetually in battle riding to arms, the Duke of Alençon. He was also closer to the Crown than by cousinship of the Blood Royal only, for he had to wife the daughter of Orleans, first cousin of the King, and her mother too was of his household. He had fought in the rout of Verneuil, five years before, and had been captured ; but when he was offered freedom if he would renounce his allegiance and swear to the Plantagenet cause, he would not, but preferred the heavy burden of his ransom.

For which loyalty his name was loved by all, and already by the Maid, though she had not seen him. He had not been in the hall on that first night when Joan had come, for he had been all day up-river in the marshes shooting quail.

He came in on the morrow, the Wednesday, and as he went to the Presence found Joan there with the King, who made them known one to the other, and she, seeing that young and comely man-at-arms, bade him welcome, saying the more of the Blood Royal were gathered about the Crown the better.

On the morrow, the Thursday, March 10th (on that day also the English about Orleans began their new stronghold, to blockade the eastern road: that great work called " The Fort of St. Loup "), he saw her again.

It was in the Castle chapel at the King's Mass, where she stood and bowed to the King; and, after mass, in that forenoon Charles took him

and La Trémoille, whose lumbering carcase was always about the King, and asked Joan also to come, and they four went together to a private room of the King's till the midday, when they dined. There it was Alençon heard the Maid speak openly of the things of France : how the Kingdom was held in fealty from God, alone of Whom Charles was Vassal and Under-Lord, as had all his fathers been before him. (For so they had stood since that day when Robert the Strong, whose father's birthplace and lineage no man knew, had held France against the heathen far back in the night of years. From him all the Kings were descended, and that Crown Capetian which was the centre and prop of the world and the eye of Christendom, now in such heavy peril.) Let Charles (she said) surrender his Fief, the great Realm, to God and receive it again in Vassalage to hold for the King of Heaven ; and let him keep to

right living in mercy, pardon prisoners, be good
to the lowly and the great and even to his
enemies.

Alençon heard her speaking and from that
day believed she was of God. And from that
day too they were fast friends in arms, under-
standing each the other.

But fat Trémoille, the fourth of that
company (himself four years on to be stabbed
and held to ransom in that same tower), was
without vision and base, he who had too much
power over the King. He was of those (and
they were the most part of the very rich men
mixed in negotiation and affairs) who knew well
the things of this world, and found it absurd,
nor even decent, that so young a girl of low
birth, unlettered, lately come from nothingness,
should play the leader, having no ground at all.
For they understood what intercourse great
gentlemen hold with their forms and manner

and their plans of state, and could read the
corrupt hearts of the rulers, and their gold,
Burgundy and Bedford and the vile queen
dowager, Anjou of Bar, Lorraine and the rest.
And their delight was in skilful play of interest
and cajole, menace and secret pact and counter-
pact : but what could she who was villein nor
even a clerk, know of such things ? With him
also in this scorn were Regnault of Chartres,
Archbishop of Rheims, Primate of the Realm
whom all must heed, and all the ruck of
the exalted. Their issue from the toils in
which the Armagnacs lay (for in their own eyes
they were but Armagnacs, and reached to no
vision of all France, the Larger Land) was to
play with Burgundy and his quarrels, wean him
from Bedford and the Plantagenets, drive
wedges into the rift. By policy and cunning
would they be saved, being hyenas laughing at
lions, and straight victory by the sword dis-

D

turbed their weavings. Nor could the King, though he was gentle and much moved by the Maid, wholly withstand them.

But Alençon believed, and the Faith in his handsome eyes remained. For he held to battle and knew the nature of war and of victory, how it is of the soul.

And now it was necessary that trial should be made of Joan's claim and of her sayings and her mission ; for men must be guarded against fraud, and even if her powers were powers indeed (as it seemed they were, for as with Baudricourt at Vaucouleurs, and as with her companions by the Meuse, so here at the Castle gate of Chinon and in hall with the King, she had knowledge and prophecy), yet must it be known, for the honour of the Crown and for its very safety, whether these powers were of Heaven or of Hell. For the men of those days were not as men now are, blind to the things

beyond the world, but knew well the strength of God and His Saints and also of the Prince of Darkness. Moreover her fame had already gone far abroad over all Christendom, and men would be writing of her in Italy and the Germanies, in Flanders and on the coasts of the sea.

Therefore many learned men and clerics as well as the great Lords came to question her in the Tower of Coudray, and messengers were sent to Domrémy to find what her people were and her childhood and character and all that could be known, but she herself was to go to Poitiers and there be examined.

For at Poitiers was a University full of learned men, both of the Church, fitted to try such things, and of the lay-learning, who could by test of question and answer sift her story thoroughly and her witness to herself. Thither had fled also such few of the great University

of Paris as still were loyal to their King. For the greater part of that mighty body, the chief doctors of the realm, held fiercely to Burgundy and the Plantagenets, hating the Armagnacs as did still the Capital wherein they sat. Therefore was Joan sent to Poitiers, not far away, two days' ride to the south, up the Vienne and the river Clain, and thither also went that doubter Regnault the Primate, and there were gathered Séguin the Dominican from the Limousin, learned in occult things, and that other Séguin the Franciscan, and Machet the King's confessor, and Aymeiri and Lombart, doctors in such things, Professors of Law and Theology, and many other clerk and lay, over whom the Primate presided.

When she was warned for the journey she knew not where they would send her, and when she heard, she sighed and said : " To Poitiers ? In God's name I shall bear burden enough—

but let us be off." For her heart was still before Orleans, and with every day its danger grew.

So she reached Poitiers and they lodged her in the house of the Advocate-General, a lay-man, Rabuteau, which house was called "The Hostel of the Rose," for in those days the private houses of principal men bore such names, and not only inns.

To her in this house came the Inquisitors in the affair and closely pressed her with question and cross-question to try out her mission and her claim. But this wearied her. For on the one side was her certain knowledge of what she had seen and heard as plainly as we see and hear the things of this world, but on the other were only words and phrases and the spinning of arguments. Also in her ears and before her eyes, frequent, returning, were those Friends of whom she was sure as of daily companions,

and their Voices no more to be mistaken than
the speech of our households. In such company
did she dwell—and the time was short. For
they had told her that she had but "a year and
a little more." And Orleans was strangling.

Yet she answered openly and with frankness,
a soul in health, and dealing with real things.
Nor was she ever moved to sharpness even at
folly, save once, when that learned Séguin
from the Limousin with his strange southern
twang and long "o's" asked her in what tongue
the Lovely Ones spoke to her—as though they
would have spoken to her in speech she could
not follow! She answered him in her clear
voice of Lorraine: "Better French than
yours!" So also when the learned Lombart
put to her again that well-worn question:
"Why did you seek the King?" she told them
that which they all knew, and, weary with such
repeating, said what she said loudly; a little

too loudly ; and to Séguin again when he asked :
" Do you believe in God ? " she made answer
with conviction : " More strongly than you ! "
for she knew that the learned are ever doubters,
peering at only one thing. The learned
Aymeiri put her the question always put to those
who assert divine aid : saying that if it were
God's will to deliver the Realm, He could do so
without men-at-arms. Whom she answered,
that if they would give her a few Knights they
would work out God's will well enough.

At last they asked her for a Sign. A Sign
she had given. But it was not for her to speak
of that secret thing, lest the King's old doubt of
his Blood should go abroad to his shame.

" Can we risk the lives of men on your bare
word ? " A miracle was demanded to confirm
such awful claims.

" In the name of God I came not here to
Poitiers to work miracles. At Orleans you will

see miracle enough. With few men or with many, to Orleans will I go."

But those days of testings and questions bore fruit. She had refused—or could not grant them then a Sign, she said. Yet a Sign she did give them, though they could not test it in that day nor in that place. It was a Sign which many then hearing lived to prove : for she prophesied.

Four things, the Maid told them in a new solemnity, four things would come to pass.

Orleans I shall relieve.

The Dauphin I shall crown in Rheims.

Paris will come back to its true King.

The Duke of Orleans, captive in the Tower of London, will return home.

In that order did she give the things to come. In that order did they come to pass.

The Court was not harsh nor opposed. They listened to her as judges and maintained their

state. Even that Primate who in his heart despised her did justice between doubt and acceptance. He admitted what might be admitted. So did they all. Some say it was because the King so willed it, some say it was because they weighed justly, being trained to such things and having no cause against her (save the feeling of the learned against the simple), and this I will believe. And all the while she was far more sure than they. Later to Alençon (to whom she told so many things) she said that she had more knowledge granted her and more power than she would own to at Poitiers ; for she was, in all her brief time, careful in the secret guardianship of her light. For though she had spoken openly of the Voices, to no one save the King had she spoken of her Visitors from Paradise. At Poitiers also she said nothing of them, and it was well that she did so, and she was rightly guided.

All that time in Poitiers whenever she spoke of Charles she called him "Dauphin" only. She who so often had called him King, to proclaim his right. They asked her why she used that word "Dauphin" which his enemies used as though to deny his crown. She answered that until *she* had crowned him, as she would, he was not King. Therefore, with these, would she use no other title.

Once again was she sent to Poitiers, but the final verdict was open enough. Let not the King reject her; so great was his peril that aid offered should not lightly be refused. Let him not take her blindly. Let him make trial of her by full knowledge of her life and by prayer, and await a Sign. . . . But the King had decided.

All these examinations were recorded. No search has discovered that record. It is lost. Or did some enemy destroy it ? After she had failed and died ?

Before death she appealed for it, but it was not brought, or her foes would not seek it. Some say that the Archbishop, never her friend, and (after she was gone from this world) her maligner, made away with the "Book of Poitiers." There is no proof. It may be that men will find it yet.

Memories of her days in Poitiers long lingered. Thibault, a lad in Rabuteau's house, remembered her, her gaiety and speech. How she clapped him on the shoulder and said she could wish for many more of such goodwill. And many years after, when all had become an ancient tale, one man lingering in the extreme of age would point out the thing he had seen in youth, by the stepping-stone at the corner of St. Stephen's Street. It was but a moment; the Maid leaping from the stone to the saddle and riding off on that Spring day when she left his town of Poitiers for the King once more, to

deliver and to crown him : for she had said :
" Indeed, for that was I born."

It was mid-April. Nearly six weeks had been
thrown away. But now the Maid could be
armed.

III

III

THEY MADE for her in Tours, by an Armourer of that town, a suit of white armour. Its plates were thick and heavy, and the helm with its vizor also was stout, and hard for a woman to wear. And there was paid for that armour as much as three hundred acres of good land will yield in rent, the worth of half a score strong horses. She had a great horse given her also to carry her, all from the King.

And there also she had made by her command a standard by which she might be known in battle. For in those days commanders needed such a thing, since with vizor lowered they could not be known by their followers save by the flag. But this standard of hers was from her

Sisters of Paradise, for it was St. Catharine and
St. Margaret who had told her, in the voices
which rapt her, of what sort it should be. It
was to be of fine white linen, with the Lilies of
the Realm scattered on it and sewn, and there
was to be painted on it the figure of Our Lord
with the world in His hand, and on either side
two angels adoring, with the motto "Jesus,
Mary." And so was it made on its long staff
for her to hold. As for the blazon on her
shield, which was blue, it was a white dove
having a scroll in its beak, and written on this
scroll were the words: "By command of the
King of Heaven."

The King would have given her a sword also,
new, as the armour was. But she had design
never to slay or wound of her own hand in
battle and would not have this sword. But
since one at-arms must have some sword, there
was given to her a sword of power: and it was

her Kin from Paradise who found it for her that she might again give a Sign.

For she had a letter written to the priests of the shrine of St. Catharine of Fierbois, the day's ride beyond Chinon, that same at which she had prayed and heard three masses in the time she was first riding to the King. There by the altar they should dig and they would find buried long in the earth, but not deep, an old sword of power. And that they might know by what authority she spoke, she told them that when they found this sword they would see graven upon it five crosses. But she did not see the man whom they sent with this message.

So they dug behind the altar of that shrine as she had commanded and found that old sword buried there in the earth, but not deeply, and the five crosses were on it, as she had said. But it was rusted. They burnished it therefore till it shone and sent it back to her at Tours.

E

And the people of Tours, glorying in this new Sign, gave her two sheaths for the sword, one of velvet for daily wearing and one in cloth of gold for great days. But she had a strong sheath of leather made for this sword and kept it therein at her side whenever she rode in arms. Yet though it was often in her hand, it never drew blood nor even struck a blow (save once when, with the flat of it, she drove from before her a loose woman of the camp), but was for her a signal of command, with which in her right hand, and the staff of her banner in her left and planted, she would stand in the heat of battle crying "*Hardi!*" to her own; to be wounded but not to wound.

And indeed, for yet another sign, she foretold the first wound she was to feel. For she told the King in those days:

"Orleans shall I save and put to flight the English, *and right on the town a shaft shall wound*

me but not mortally, and this very summer shall you be crowned in Rheims."

And this she said in mid-April, when she was returned from Poitiers to be armed.

Now there was in the city of Lyons at that time one Rotselaer, a merchant from Flanders who was serving princes and cities in the plots of those times. And as all were now speaking of the Maid throughout the West and all Christendom, so in the Low Countries (which were Burgundy's), whence Rotselaer came, her cause was much debated, for and against. Therefore this man wrote a letter to them, from Lyons, to Brussels in Brabant, which is the chief town of those parts. This letter he marked with the day of writing, which was Friday the twenty-second day of April, and in it he told what the Maid had said to the King, how she would be wounded by a shaft before Orleans, but not mortally ; for the fame of this fore-

telling had reached the place where he lay. This letter was put on record by the Recorder of the Treasury of Brussels and so bore witness.

It happened that in these same days of April her brothers John and Peter came to join her (for they had been on Pilgrimage with their mother from Domrémy to the shrine of Our Lady of Le Puy in the mountains), and with them was the Priest Pasquerel who became her chaplain ; and all these joined her household, to which also was now added another page-boy, Raymond, with the Knight John d'Aulnon and her constant attendants Nouillonpont and Poulengy, who had ridden with her from the marches of Lorraine.

And now she would set out. But before she did so she sent to Bedford, the chief of the English, and to the Enemy before Orleans, a Summons, as was the custom of Christendom, so that blood should not be shed unduly in a

wrong cause. This was the Summons which
she had spoken word for word in Poitiers on
the Tuesday in Holy Week near a month ago,
and had had written down for her and had
signed :

"King of England, and you, Duke of
Bethfort who call yourself regent of the Realm
of France ; William de la Poule Earl of Suffort,
John Lord of Thelabot and you, Thomas, Lord
of Escalles who call yourselves Lieutenants of
the said Duke of Bethfort, do right by the King
of Heaven to the Blood Royal : yield to the
Maid who is sent of God, the King of Heaven,
the keys of all the good towns you have taken
and ravished in France. She has come hither
by orders of the King of Heaven to redeem the
Blood Royal ; she is ready to make peace if you
will do right by her and by France, to which
you may do justice and repay what you have

seized. And you, Archers and Barrack-room companions of war, of high birth or of low, who stand before the good town of Orleans, be off, in the name of God, to your own Country. King of England, if you will not do so, I am a Leader in War and in whatever place I may find your folk in France I will turn them out willy-nilly, and who will not obey I shall kill and who will obey I shall spare. Nor believe that you can hold aught of the Realm of France. No, by God, the Son of Mary! Charles the King will hold it, the right heir. For God the King of Heaven wills it so, as the Maid has revealed to him. He will come at last into Paris with a goodly company. If you will not hearken to the words of God by the mouth of the Maid, in whatever place we find you we will strike great swinges and make such a rough-and-tumble as has not been raised in France this thousand years. Then shall we see which has

better right from the God of Heaven, we or you!"

And when, later, she had come to Orleans, two heralds bore this Summons. One, the Commanders of the Siege-Army sent back; the other (Guienne was his name) they kept, saying they would burn him—yes, and if they caught her, the Maid too: who on hearing it said: "Let them burn me if they ever hold me, but if I have the victory, let them be gone." Yet they held her at the last.

Before attack could be made, first it was thought better to provision the town, and for this a great convoy was made ready down river, at Blois, a town in the King's power, distant from Orleans three days' march, in marches of a dozen miles, but at one long day's riding. And the reason it was thought better to provision the town was this:

Already some time past, the Duke of Burgundy having taken his men away on an excuse (he had not broken with Bedford, but he played fast and loose, listening to the intrigues at Chinon, and watching where his best advantage might lie), the English commanders had sent for reinforcement. And, being now free to do as they would without tampering from Burgundy (who claimed the place and who might have spared it), they determined to reduce it without further delay. Moreover, as they were not numerous enough to make sure of assault upon so large a city, they would starve it into surrender. Hitherto they had watched it only on the side whence succour might come, that is, from the west, down river, looking towards Chinon and Tours ; and so by other parts food could reach the besieged. But now they put up works on the east also and made the blockade straighter ; and soon, when more men should

reach them they would make it complete. So there was little time in which to relieve the city.

And now it must be seen how this town of Orleans lay.

It is upon the river Loire, which was then, before new wharves were made, about two furlongs wide or a little more from bank to bank. The Loire comes here from the east and flows westwards, and it is on the North Bank that Orleans stands. It was large for a city of those days, being near five furlongs or more from the river to the North Gate where the Paris road went out, and seven at the least from the eastern to the western side along the river : that is, measuring from the outermost of the ditch, but less from wall to wall.

The river Loire which supplied it is not as other rivers in France of the North. For these are full and still all the year, but the Loire runs

very high and full or very shallow, all in a few
days, according as rains have fallen, or the snows
have melted in the mountains far off to the
south where it rises. Should you see it in the
end of a long Summer drought you would think
it hardly a river at all, only trickles of water
between great sand-banks which fill its bed.
But after rains it runs so much higher that it
would hide a house : but not for long. The
rains ceasing the water runs quickly away. Such
strangeness in the river has also this trouble
about it : that when it is fitted to carry large
boats, then is it a raging current against which
only a strong wind will carry vessels upwards,
and when the current is slack, why then there
is no water for deep craft. Now the French
forces lay downstream, and to move goods by
river to Orleans they must breast the current.

From Orleans to the opposite bank on the
south the great road was carried by a bridge

built more than two hundred years before the days of the Maid, and this bridge the men of Orleans had broken at the arches of its southern end, to prevent the enemy from entering by it. And at that southern end, on the right bank the English had strengthened and held the two stone towers that defended it, called "The Tourelles," and had dug a moat in front of them, leading the river water through and passing this moat by a drawbridge, and on the far side of this drawbridge a little way inland they had put up a bastion, palisaded, to make a further protection ; and beyond this again they had their fort called " of the Augustinians."

As for their other works they were many, but the chief ones were four. A stronghold of mound and palisade west of the town near the river, called " St. Laurence," and watching the road from Blois and down river. Another to the north called " Paris," because it watched

the Paris road. Then that one to the south (opposite the Tourelles and the Bastion) called the "Augustinians," from a ruined Monastery on which it was built, and watching the road from the south : and lately the English had also built in the east, up river, a very large one called "St. Loup," from the suburb where it lay. It watched the road from the east and from up river.

Such was the setting of the besieging army round Orleans, but we must understand both that there were other works in between these, making a ring, and yet that the number of besiegers so far had never been enough to prevent provisions coming in sometimes through the gaps between the strong-points. Also by holding so many scattered forts they had not yet enough in any one of them to beat off any large body attempting to enter the town ; but they were expecting new forces and already they had

so much blocked the roads that food was growing scarce and would soon be scarcer still.

On Thursday the twenty-eighth day of April, then, the Thursday before Ascension Week, this convoy was gathered at Blois to revictual Orleans.

A large column went with it ; of fighting men equipped and disciplined perhaps not more than four thousand, but with them many more of rough levies ; chance zealots also, and the clergy in a great band chanting the " Veni Creator." At their head rode Joan with standard and page, in her white armour which on that day of her arrival before Orleans (it was Thursday the twenty-eighth of April) she wore for the first time during so many hours.

They went by the southern bank, to her anger. For she had wished to go by the northern and so come straight on the town. The Captains had thwarted that plan ; for the

enemy held Beaugency and Meung in between, and their main camp was by the river outside the western gate of the city. She had said that the English would not sally out from their forts or their camp—and she was right: for their strength in small detachments was not sufficient and they trusted, for reducing the city, to their guns, for the moment, and next to the reinforcement coming in few days. Had the Maid ridden in that day she would have satisfied her heart in its zeal.

Therefore, when he who commanded the garrison of Orleans crossed over the water to meet her on the southern bank she was still angered, and asked him why the change had been made.

He told her the wisest Captains had thought it best. She answered: "They who guide me are wiser far."

He was the Bastard of Orleans, half-brother

of the Duke who lay prisoner in England, and uncle of Alençon's wife. Later he was to be called Count of Dunois—and from the first he believed in the Maid, for he was a soldier. But there was that to come, within the hour, which was to make him believe more firmly.

The boats loaded with the provisionment for Orleans lay by the shore. They were planned to go up stream five miles to Chécy village and thence their cargoes were to come by road to the Eastern Gate called "the Burgundian." For by the Western Gate the enemy were more numerous, but here, on the east, only the fort of St. Loup with three hundred men, threatened the highway : and that could be covered by such forces as would be ferried over.

But to get the laden boats up these five miles against the strong stream was not possible, for a strong wind blew down river from the east where Chécy lay.

When, therefore, the Bastard had told her
that the wisdom of the Captains had thwarted
her plan and she had answered him, she used
also these words :

"You are deceived—better succour do I
bring than ever yet came to town or man-at-
arms, for it is the aid of the King of Heaven."

And immediately that east wind fell, and
after a pause it blew suddenly and with violence
from the west ; nor could the Bastard in nearly
thirty years efface that moment from his mind.
But in his age he bore testimony to the awe
that came on him, calling what had passed a
Miracle of God.

For the wind was now so violent from the
west that each barge under sail could tow two
others, and all came that day to Chécy, where
no man after the morning had hoped to see
them, and Joan crossed with two hundred lances
and slept that Thursday night at Reilly close

at hand, in the house of one Guy de Chailly, of whom this is told : that alone of mortals before or since he, in that night, was granted vision of the Celestials about her and was shaken.

On the next day, the Friday, they would have her hold hard in Reilly during the light ; but when darkness had fallen, an hour after sunset, she rode out at the Bastard's right hand, splendidly horsed, and saw, as she came near the Burgundian Gate, great light of many torches and heard the noise of a crowd, for the city was pouring out to meet her. She had changed men's hearts ; the citizen levies would now move ; the garrison no longer feared ; the men-at-arms smelt victory ; and in Talbot's command was gathering the dread of unearthly things. They thought Joan leagued with dreadful powers and their spirits failed.

As she came in through the streets to the

F

shouting of the people, and their press and the glare of torches, women and men and little children surging against her stirrups to touch and kiss her mail, a flame caught her Standard. She turned the staff down to let the embroidered thing touch the ground and moved her horse over it to crush out the flame, then raised it again.

They passed on slowly in their shouting thousands to the Church of the True Cross to give thanks, and then bore her to the house of Boucher, the Duke's treasurer, by the Western Gate called " Regnart " on the far side of the city. She had traversed it from end to end, and already in spirit the cause was won.

Next day she summoned Glasdale in the Tourelles, promising peace. But they mocked her for a peasant ; then all Sunday, May-day, and the morrow also and the next day too she waited, the cheering crowd about her house ;

for the Bastard and his troops were off to meet
a new convoy. On the Wednesday they came
in by morning with the provisions and she rode
out with her men to meet them. But when
she returned she was wearied by her armour
and lay down to rest, her hostess by her, while
on a couch in that room lay D'Aulnon her
Knight.

She slept. But her Voices called her and
woke her. She cried to her companions that
there was fighting afoot. She cursed her
page for letting her sleep on. She hastened
into her armour, shouting for her horse, and
when she was mounted, she called at the street
door for her Standard, which in her haste she
had left behind, and the lad gave it through a
window : then she galloped off with D'Aulnon
to the Eastern Gate, the sparks flying from the
horse-shoes until, with sure knowledge, she
came to where, two miles away, the Bastard's

men were thundering round the works of St. Loup ; whom she joined, till the fort was taken and all the English in it taken or slain.

Time pressed. They had news that Fastolf and his English reinforcements were far advanced towards Orleans on the Paris road. That night—it was the fourth of May—she said that *within five days* the siege would be raised : that is, by the eighth.

But once more Joan would summon the Tourelles. She went perilously along the bridge to where the broken arches were and had her message shot by an arrow into the English hold. But those who took it up cried back: "News from the Armagnac's Whore!" at which word she wept : but her Divine Ones comforted her.

The next day was Thursday, the Feast of the Ascension, and a truce of arms. Upon the morrow, the Friday, did the triumph begin.

If the southern post beyond the river, the Tourelles, should fall, the siege was broken; since, should that go, there would be thenceforward all the river front open for access to the town. She bade them wake her at dawn.

On this southern bank was that main fort of the Besiegers, the Augustinians, guarding the southern road to the bridge with a smaller fort to one side: between it and the bridge the Rampart thrown out to guard the Tourelles, behind the Rampart again, on the water-side at the end of the bridge overlooking the broken arches, the stone towers of the Tourelles themselves; Glasdale holding them.

First on that Friday morning the town militia crossed, up river, and Glasdale withdrew his men from the side-fort and massed on the Augustinians, whence a sally threw the townsmen back in a herd. But at that moment did the Maid herself land and rally them. She,

D'Aulnon, and the gentlemen-at-arms now landed, mounted, charged with lances and, not without confusion, the foot-levies charged in turn upon the gate of the Augustinians, such mettle had the fire of those days put into them, and Joan's coming. Before her in a great press the struggle swayed ; with which she mingled until, at long last, the Augustinians fell and with it all the men therein were taken or killed. In that day, in the heat of it, she had dismounted, urging them on, and her foot was hurt on a caltrop. She crossed back to Orleans for the victory of the morrow when the Tourelles themselves should fall, and though it was Friday she broke her fast, for the armour had oppressed her, and the thunder of battle all those hours.

In the first hours of the morning of that great morrow, Saturday the seventh day of May, she heard her mass and going out in harness

she said to her chaplain: "This day shall I be wounded, above the left breast. Yet shall I return: and by the bridge." At which last words he wondered the more: for the bridge was broken.

So she rode out and crossed by water to the farther shore where the victors of the eve had bivouacked in the fields. The Bastard was with her, La Hire, all the Captains; and within the Tourelles or holding the Rampart without, six hundred: English of the English. For upon the roll of Glasdale and his captains were such names as these: Tom Reid, Pat Hull, Jack Burford, Dick Hawke, Tom Jolly, Black Harry, Hall, and Sand.

Hour upon hour of that morning the stone walls of the Rampart swarmed with scaling ladders full of men hurled down, and assault upon assault repelled, and the Maid in the midst with her banner; when, at noon, a shaft

struck right through the white shoulder plate over her left breast and she fell.

They dressed the wound with oil ; before the reddening of the day she had returned. But though the struggle still raged, the sun set upon the place unconquered, and Talbot watching from beyond the river could make sure that it had held. " We soldiers made sure that the place was unconquerable." Had it not been held till this close of day ? And Talbot beyond the river heard the Bastard's trumpets sounding the recall.

But Joan went into a field apart to pray : and having prayed she urged the Commander, the Bastard, till though darkness was falling, he gave counter-orders and called for a last surge against that stone. In the ditch of the moat D'Aulnon handed her Standard to a Basque to hold. As this went down the slope and the Rampart hid it she thought it lost, and coming

forward she went into the ditch and grasped it, and struggled on with the others towards the wall. They could see the white of that Standard in the gloom, and she cried loudly : " When the flag touches the stone, all is yours ! " And as the white of it touched the wall in the half-light the defence crashed and the assault poured in. Over the burning drawbridge the men flying for the Tourelles stumbled and were drowned (their leader Glasdale among them), save some few who ran through to the towers. Beyond the Tourelles a narrow plank-way had been thrust over the gap of broken arches and the towers were surrounded. They fell as it was night, and all within were taken or slain.

So Joan, wounded, came by the bridge in the darkness to Orleans freed, and Talbot heard the bells ringing through the night and knew what had befallen, and that Orleans was lost to him.

IV

IV

WHEN THESE things had been done and Orleans freed, the English host withdrew from the forts remaining, and next day set themselves out in battle on the plain. But in a little while they turned about and were gone; and though the French would have attacked, the Maid forbade them saying: "You will have them upon a coming day." But still they held walled towns upon the river above and below: Jargeau and Meung and Beaugency, with bridge and bridgehead beyond, upon the southern shore. And thereby, should help come to them, they might cross the Loire in strength into Charles's land and perhaps overcome him yet.

Therefore would Joan have carried those cities and bridges at once and stormed them, and when they were taken march straight to Rheims for the crowning and anointing of the King.

But the court delayed ; for they still ensnared themselves in nets of high policy and thought to make all well by treaties with Burgundy, for men said truly : " If Burgundy abandon Bedford, soon there will not be left one fighting Englishman in all France." But Burgundy, that strong Prince, holding all the eastern part of the realm of right, and having also the rich towns of the Netherlands and their merchandise, could bide his time, and was far more cunning than they. So he still played them and the English Captains, and Bedford their Regent, one against the others as a Master in chess plays pieces on the board : saying in his heart : " I will make each so eager for me that each will do

my will. So at last I will be master over my own Country, and have no King over me at all, whether my cousin the Valois, or the Plantagenet. And my children after me will rule an eastern realm of their own in full sovereignty." And indeed in his leisure he chose at a later time to make a truce with Charles, but only for a set time and to a day fixed, nor did he take arms against Bedford, so that he still held them both.

Also that false counsellor, La Trémoille, kept back the gentle King, despising the Maid ; and because he had a quarrel with Richemont, the great soldier, Brother of Brittany, and Constable, he kept off the force which that Captain led, and would not have Charles use it for the recovery of his throne. And though Charles had given his kingly word that he would take back Richemont, yet did La Trémoille make him break that word, for he had the Dauphin in debt to him and fearful of him too.

And Richemont and all his men were shut off
from the King lest he should supplant La
Trémoille in power over the King's mind.

But Joan was fevered at such lingering,
knowing that she had but a year. Also her
Voices bade her urgently to march ; and the
High Ones of Heaven are wiser than men.

So, on a day, while they were still plotting at
Loches, she came with the Bastard of Orleans,
and knocked at the door of the Council Room,
and coming in fell before the King and clasped
his knees, saying : "Dauphin, noble Dauphin,
linger not here in council with many words, but
come to Rheims and be crowned. For the
Voice calls to me, 'Go forward, Daughter of
God ; I am with you. Go ! Go !'"

At last then, persuaded, the timid Valois
gave royal orders that the towns should be
cleared, but already it was a month gone since
the great day of Orleans. For only on Thurs-

day the ninth day of June did they set out, the
Bastard of Orleans and Alençon and Joan with
her knights, D'Aulnon and her page, and all her
company and the host about her. And with
them were two young men of Brittany, high
born, Guy, and Andrew, son of the Lord of
Laval in Brittany, whose fathers had been Lords
of that tall keep and town for fourteen genera-
tions, famous men. They and so many had
come in to Charles's aid without summons, in
honour of the Maid. For it was the young who
loved her and knew her to be of Heaven.

It was at Selles, in Berry, that they had met,
and there, as she poured out wine for them and
drank with them, she said merrily : " Soon you
(or we) will drink in Paris yet ! " And they saw
that she was divine.

Also they wrote at the time the things that
had passed at their meeting : how Joan stood
bravely at the doors in her white armour, but

G

unhelmeted, having lance and pennant and a little steel axe for badge of command in her right hand. How, also, a great black charger was brought for her to mount, and how the horse pawed and reared, not be to managed. And how she said: "Take him to the Cross there before us by the Church." Where the charger stood stock-still for her to mount; and so she rode away north to Orleans and all the men-at-arms about her.

First they would carry Jargeau. But before Jargeau, the French had already failed, not having the Maid amongst them, and now again the Captains feared it would stand and its walls hold. But Fastolf on the same day had left Paris with reinforcement for Jargeau, where Suffolk commanded, and Fastolf had under his command many guns, and provision to relieve the town, so it must be taken now or never.

Now Jargeau was from Orleans two days'

march away up the river-side, so going out on the Thursday, they came before it on the Saturday, the eleventh of June, before evening, and the Maid summoned the town. Some would have had parley, and have let the garrison go free if Suffolk would yield the town, but Joan on the morrow, the Sunday, stood to see the firing of the great gun brought from Orleans, and when, by the battering of it, a tower fell, Alençon dreaded the breach, thinking it not wide enough yet and too high piled with stone ; but she said to him : " To the Breach and fear nothing ! This is the hour of God's pleasure ; and do you not remember how I told your wife in Tours, that I would bring you home ? "

And she herself ran forward, while Suffolk on the wall would still parley. And she had her foot on the scaling ladder when a stone struck her on the helm and felled her ; but she rose to her feet and cried : " On, Friends, on !

Hearts high! We have them in this hour!"
And the town was carried, the garrison, flying
for the bridges, was slaughtered in the pursuit
and Suffolk himself taken captive: and that
evening Alençon and the Maid rode back in
triumph to Orleans, all the long way, with the
footmen following.

Then in great haste she would take Meung
also upon the western road, downstream, and
on the day after the morrow, the Tuesday (the
footmen having come marching in upon the eve,
their two days' march from Jargeau), she would
not hold, but used the flame of the time, and
said to Alençon: "To-morrow, after the meal
at midday, we must all for Meung. Give
orders." So on that Thursday they set out
again all confident, she in a fine coat of Cramoisy
(that is, Deep Red) and of Dark Green over her
white armour, which coat (being his colours)
the prisoner Duke of Orleans had paid for in

her honour with thirteen pieces of gold, a cloth worth many horses. And on that same day at evening they carried the bridgehead and held it, and the very next day, unwearied, pressed on to Beaugency farther down the stream.

But the garrison in Beaugency, seeing Richemont come up in aid of the French and much outnumbering them, abandoned the town and bridge and took to the Castle. Yet some among the French Captains were still for holding Richemont off and refusing his aid, since by the pressing of Richemont's enemy La Trémoille the King had ordered it : but Joan received Richemont, loving his manner and his soldiership. For he had said : " Joan, they say you would repel me. Now whether you are from God or the Devil I know not. But if from God I fear nothing, for He knows my heart is loyal ; but if from the Devil, then I

fear you not at all." And that night the Castle surrendered.

Now the next day, Friday of that week of glories, news came by patrols galloping in that the great Talbot was returning with a new host to succour Beaugency which he did not know had fallen, and that he was a day's march or a little more to the north, marching forward. And so terrible was his name that many feared to meet him and would have fallen back. And so it was also in Talbot's camp, where Fastolf had joined him : for Fastolf thought the enemy too strong, and his men were shaken ; knowing the fall of Jargeau (though not yet of Beaugency) and dreading beyond all things what they took for the incantations of the Maid, whom they believed a sorceress and in league with Hell ; as now did Bedford too and all the English. But Talbot had said : " By God and St. George ! I will attack." So he went

forward, a mighty captain, dedicated to the life of war, and to fall in white hairs, very old, twenty years on in the last charge of his people, to southward, by Chastillon far away.

And in the French camp also Joan urged them on, crying: "In the name of God, we must fight them! Were they hanging from the clouds we yet should drag them down." And that evening she stood with her host upon a little hill which rises there out of the plain, and when the sun was low they drew up in order on that height waiting for the morrow, with the English host not far off but unseen, for there were many woods about and high hedges. Before it was night heralds came in from the English offering duels of three knights against three, for an ordeal, to abide by the issue. But those about the Maid gave them this answer from her: "Go to your rest: to-morrow, we shall see you close enough, if God and Our

Lady will." And later she said to those of her company : " Have you good spurs ? " " Why ? " they answered, " to fly ? " " No ! " she said, " to pursue."

The next morning Talbot and Fastolf fell back towards the Paris road (whether for better position or because they might find reinforcement, or from advice of too great strength against them we do not know), while Joan and her army went on northward, still finding nothing in that blind country of copse and high hedgerow where the enemy was, till they saw before them the spire of Lignerolles village and to the left a town called Patay, small but a market, from which place the battle that was to come took its name. And all the while the enemy went before them unseen, having at the head a knight with a white standard, next to him the guns and the many waggons, then the levies of Picardy, and others of the north who

were under the Burgundian and Plantagenet allegiance ; and last, by way of rear-guard, where the danger lay, a picked body, all English.

Now Talbot, knowing that the French were at hand (though they had not yet seen one of his men, so well had he chosen cover for his march), picked out a force of chosen archers— for the English bow had long been invincible— and set them out with orders to fix their stakes before them hidden behind a tall thick hedge, that so they might let fly at the first line of his foes where they should come. But Fastolf's body were yet some little way off. And it happened that the French horsemen, scouting forward, started a stag in a thicket, which bounded towards the hedges behind which those English archers were hidden, still making ready their stakes, but having not yet fixed them. Now when the archers peering through the

hedgerow saw the stag, they, loving sport, raised the View-Halloa, and the French scouts in the wood hearing it, knew their prey : they had found !

So they rode back at speed and warned their Captains, and in a moment, the French men-at-arms were deployed and came charging down upon those archers unprepared, and broke them to pieces.

Yet was this but one line and but a tenth of the whole body, though the best ; and Fastolf, coming up before his footmen, with the main mounted force, galloped hard to join the men who were behind the archers and whom the knight with the white standard led. But he that held the white standard, seeing the dust and the charge coming up, thought it was the enemy come upon him and his body unawares, so he withdrew, and Fastolf's galloping line, when they drew rein, found themselves on the

field alone, and their footmen far outdistanced, and all the French host before them. Thereupon those round Fastolf said to him that to offer battle was madness. He himself would have stood and gone down, but they drew him away; and the enemy seeing such confusion, charged again all in line with their lances set, and destroyed the footmen all, and such of the cavalry as were standing, and they were utterly overthrown.

In that day of Patay, Saturday the eighteenth of June, for the first time were the Plantagenet's ranks defeated in the open field and it was of heavy augury. The guns were lost and the long baggage train, and of the whole army of that morning, not one man in five but was taken or slain.

Talbot himself being led captive before Alençon, that young soldier, who remembered his own seizing at Verneuil, five years past,

and the heavy ransom he had paid, said to Talbot :

" This morning you did not think to see such things ? "

But Talbot answered, " *Fortune de guerre*."

Yet Talbot, later, Alençon let go free without ransom ; so greatly did he revere that captain.

Fastolf, coming to Bedford at Corbeuil, told all, and they stripped him of his Garter, and his name has been a mockery from that day on : but unjustly.

That night Joan slept in Lignerolles and next day she and the Army with her rode back into Orleans, where the townsfolk roared victory and beflagged the street, and all believed that the Dauphin would come and from that town march on at once for Rheims.

But even now the Court still hung in doubt of policy. For between Rheims and them were

strong walled cities, which the Burgundians held, and maybe could still hold against them, or perhaps in time would share if they should at last make terms with Burgundy : Auxerre and Troyes and Chalons, and Rheims itself, a well-walled city, and many castles. They thought also of their lack of provision and treasure for a march across near a hundred leagues of land. And all this the false La Trémoille recited, delaying the King at Sully his home.

Therefore did Charles not set out for Orleans, but Joan must go seek him ; and they met at St. Benedict's on the Loire, and there Joan besought him to go forward at once to the crowning. For, as she had told him after first they met, St. Louis and St. Charlemagne were praying on their knees before the Throne of God for him, of the Blood Royal, to whom, anointed, all the Realm would fall, till France

was restored in splendour, and Christendom at rest from wars.

To whom, so pleading, the gentle Dauphin, disturbed, could only give great thanks for her marvels and her shining victories, and said that she should repose a while from so much toil. But at last she moved him, and he set out for Gien, thence to start north upon his road.

Yet at Gien for a week and more they lingered —it may be that money must be gathered or provisioning—which they lacked sorely and were to lack throughout that advance—or that, men coming in from the countrysides on hearing of the movement and for honour of the Maid, they wanted to swell their numbers. For every day would ride into Gien the gentlemen from their manors here and there, and knights-adventurers, and companies of men ; but of pay they could have little or none. And during all

those days Joan chafed as a river that is held back
in storm by trees fallen, or as a hound in leash
that strains at the groom's holding, until, upon
a Sunday (it was the twenty-sixth day of June)
she knew that the advance was at hand, and on
the next day she rode out herself joyfully
northwards with her men, her face set for
Rheims, and with her the host, her Knight
D'Aulnon and Alençon and the Bastard, and all
the Companions, La Hire and the young pages,
and she with the standard in her hand : day
by day at the rate of the footmen. And two
days later the Dauphin rode out with his household to join them, and all the army was on the
march for Rheims. Till they came to the first
strong town upon their way, and once again
Joan saw, in their broad valley of summer
meadows new shorn from the scythe, the red
tiles of Auxerre and the stone walls about it as
she had seen them under the winter weather,

three months gone, in those first days when she was riding from Domrémy to find her King.

Now Auxerre was a town under allegiance to Burgundy, but it would have yielded. And the Maid could have taken it had it refused. But secretly the false La Trémoille had taken two thousand pieces of gold to spare it, and he showed how it was best to deal gently with Burgundians. So she was overruled. But the city consented to sell food which the host must have, and so again after three days they went forward leaving it behind.

And next they came to the countryside round Troyes, the chief city on their way. Stronger than Auxerre by far, and with great walls and populous, and having a garrison of the Burgundians with some English also. They lay before it at St. Phal on July the fourth at evening, and on the next morning the Maid sent them

summons, in the name of the King of Heaven, that they should render allegiance to the true King who would at last hold all the cities of Holy France his Realm, and so make lasting peace. But the burghers of Troyes were boastful and said they had sworn on the Body of the Lord that never would they yield the town.

Now there was in Troyes at that time a Franciscan, called Brother Richard, who wrought wonders and said that Doomsday was at hand. Some called him mad but others holy. This man went out from the city towards the Maid making signs of the Cross and sprinkling holy water, lest she should have evil powers. But she laughed and said : " Come on without fear ! " and so persuaded him that he went back within the gates of Troyes and preached to the people that they should give her the town. But they would not : talking very big, and knowing that

H

the King had no siege train and was needing bread.

In this halt, four days after they had come before the city, the King held council, and Regnault the Primate Archbishop of Rheims spoke for retreat. They had come near a hundred miles from Gien, their food was low and they had no treasure, and if Auxerre could not be taken, how could Troyes fall, which was one of the strongest cities of the world ? But one there in the Council, Macon, who had been Chancellor in his time, bade them send for the Maid, who said, on hearing their arguments :

" High-born Dauphin, do you give credence to this ? Wait but two days and the town is yours."

Said the Primate : " We could last just six— if we were sure." But she bade them have faith.

Then for all that day, which was the eighth of July, she went about the host and all that night and all the morrow, rousing them like a swarm of bees to labour together with zeal and rumour, and to make fascines, and wooden shields for the assault and to gather such provision as remained, and the next day again—the tenth, a Sunday—she came to the moat with her standard, crying "At them!" and gave the order to cast forward the fascines and fill the ditch. But at the coming of the stroke, the heart of the townsmen failed them (their Bishop also secretly favoured the true King) and in that same hour they yielded; so, as the Dauphin's host came in by the western gate, the garrison marched out by the eastern, and Troyes was theirs, and replenishment; and its strength no longer barred the road.

After Troyes all was clear. For Chalons, Troyes having fallen, yielded gladly enough;

and Rheims, next on, two days away, was ready to admit the King.

On Saturday the sixteenth of that month, the host lay before the Sacred City of the Crowning, and the Dauphin in Sept-Saulx, the village of the willows on the chalky stream, whence the square towers of that Cathedral stand up to the north against the sky.

The Sunday, the seventeenth day of July in the year of Our Lord fourteen hundred and twenty-nine, the Dauphin Charles rode in with his company for the crowning, while all the people in the streets cried "*Noël!*" And the father of Joan, James of Arc, had come there, lying at the inn of the Striped Donkey in the Cathedral square, and men and women from all the country round.

Right into the High Church through the great doors wide open rode Charles, still mounted, and all his company with him up to

the steps of the choir, and there was he anointed and crowned King amid the shouts of the people and the trumpets sounding in the vaults, and beside him stood Joan with the standard.

But when he was crowned and anointed, and King indeed at last, she knelt at his feet with strong and many tears, and said :

"High-born King, now is the Will of God accomplished. For He it was Who ordained that I should free Orleans and bring you here to this City of Rheims for your Sacring, to blazon it forth that you are Rightful Lord. And now the Realm of France is yours."

V

V

NOW FROM Rheims the Maid would have marched that army to Paris, a week away, or a little more. For Paris was the head and captain of the Realm, the King's town of all France; and he that held it was manifestly Chief and Lord. So that men still say the host should have made right for Paris after the Triumph of Patay and perhaps have entered, seeing that the enemy after that slaughter and rout were shaken to their marrow and thought all Hell had risen up against them with Joan for its servant. But the Voices had ordered that Rheims should come first, and the Crowning, for They knew in their wisdom that by the spirit all is decided, and now was the King anointed and on that

Sacrament could full victory be built; but slowly, after twenty years.

Also, after the trumpets had sounded and the great Church was silent, the Voices never more gave orders for the field; but all Joan did thenceforward, or desired and counselled for the setting of the war, came from herself alone, uncertainly. Since from the beginnings in Domrémy, They had said: "Raise you the siege of Orleans and crown your Prince in Rheims." But of battle beyond They had said nothing. Yet were her Brethren of Paradise in full communion with her, sustaining her through the evils of this world, and she still conversed with Them, seeing Them with her eyes, and she was supported by Their shining presence at the end.

In Rheims the King lingered, four days and five; the Court about him still set on policy and the winning over of Burgundy to their

side, and weaning him from the Plantagenet, from the boy Henry of England, and Bedford's rule : thinking this could be done and not seeing that Burgundy was the more cunning.

Then they set out, but deviously, not making straight down the Paris road, nor having Joan to the Council. They passed to Soissons and received that town and then to Château-Thierry, where was a bridge with towers that gave passage over the Marne river, across which bridge the King and his army went as though to make for the south again, in spite of the Maid's urging, and to rely on peace by words with Burgundy rather than by arms : for Burgundy still parleyed to deceive them, and made a truce of fifteen days, and talked of yielding Paris to them without battle.

And they went on still southwards and away from Paris to receive the strong town of Provins, and still went southward. But, barring

their way, an English force had seized the
bridge of Bray over the river Seine. So they
turned north again and came to Crépy in the
Valois and to Ferté by the great wood.

As for Paris itself, they put it off in their
minds; though openly they did not speak so,
but said in their hearts: "The place is very
large and strong, much more in circuit than any
other town of France, so that siege we cannot
lay, being so few and with no machines for
battery nor great guns but only small. Also
within those walls the myriads of the City hate
us for Armagnacs still, and cling to Burgundy.
Let us wait till the City falls to us through his
friendship."

But Joan, now that perforce the army had
been faced north again, believed that Paris
they would attain, and therefore she could
write to them of Rheims, who were grown full
of foreboding at the Court's delays:

" Good friends and loyal men of France and true, the Maid sends you news of herself that never in life will she abandon you. Written from the road to Paris."

In those days—and now from the Crowning nearly a month had gone by—as she was riding between the Bastard of Orleans and Regnault the Archbishop, she said in her joy at the people's cheering for the King : " Here are good folk, and here would I lie buried in this earth of theirs, when I die." But never was she to lie at peace in Christian earth beside the Blessed Dead, but more brightly, through the fire, to strike to Paradise. Regnault said to her :

" And where, Joan, do you think to die ? "

To whom she answered :

" When God wills. The place and hour I know not more than you. Ah, that God would let me now, now, lay down arms and go back to

my father and my mother to minister to them and to fold their sheep ! " For she saw within her heart the valley where she was born and the young Meuse flowing by.

The Bastard of Orleans, riding at her further rein, who had known her for what she was from that day when he had first found her, in white armour, over against Orleans by the riverside, said to himself : " Her mission is accomplished." But whether she herself knew this, no man can tell.

Next day they came near to Senlis, and there they found, on the feast of the Assumption of Our Lady, the English in a camp, fortified with a Palisade ; and already Bedford had sent a challenge most insolent, calling Charles, " you that style yourself King," and saying of the Maid that she was a woman of loose life and a harlot. For he raged against her that the realm should be slipping from his hand ; and

his party called her a witch, and he himself called her a member of Satan, and they had said often and again that should she fall to them they would burn her. When Bedford thus challenged he had hoped that the King's force would waste itself against an enemy entrenched and guarded, as they had spent and spilt themselves in disaster at Rouvray months ago, before the coming of the Maid. They fell into no such folly on that day. But Joan rode forward to the Palisade and struck it with her sword.

When the English host had departed, Senlis gladly received the King, and Beauvais too, from which town Peter Cauchon, its Bishop, fled, swearing to be avenged; for he was a great man in the cause of the Plantagenets, and later, through him, was the Maid to die.

But more than Beauvais or Senlis and of chief import to the right Cause, Compiègne, that strong city, gave itself also gladly to the

King, and of how it was Compiègne that served
and saved the Crown in its own despite we shall
come to later on.

Upon the 23rd of August Alençon with a good
band of knights left Charles in Compiègne, and
set forth at last for Paris, having with him the
Maid ; who in her joy said, riding forward :
" By my Distaff ! I would see Paris closer at
hand ! " And on the fourth day they came to
St. Denis, without the walls, where is the Shrine
of the Oriflamme the sacred Banner of the
Realm, and where the Kings of France lie buried
beneath the diadem of Charlemagne. There
did the men of Alençon's command and the
Maid with them make a stay, gathering fascines
and other matter as though for an assault on the
wall of Paris, wherein lay the armed men of
Burgundy, and some few score of English bearing
the banner of St. George. Yet did the Court
of King Charles not desire to take the town, but

to let young Alençon in his zeal make demonstration there with the Maid to appease her: but secretly they planned otherwise.

For this is what they had done. Still in their folly they had once more sought peace through Burgundy and had made a new truce with him to last all that year, and it was added to, until Easter of the next. And they had said that Burgundy might hold Paris, in the hope of making him their friend at last, and had even told him he might garrison Compiègne. But they of Compiègne would have none of a Burgundian force within their walls, seeing more clearly than saw Charles's advisers.

This thing also happened at St. Denis in those days. Joan's sword, the sword from St. Catherine of Fierbois, was broken by mischance.

It was upon Thursday, the eighth day of September of that year fourteen hundred and twenty-nine, being the birthday of the Mother

I

of God, that the doomed assault began : but
tardily. Not till mid-morning did they set
out, and not till the second hour after noon
were the guns sounding : but from far off, nor
were those guns of a size to break the wall.

When, therefore, the Maid and Alençon
came, with too few men about them, to the
St. Honoré Gate of Paris, it was very late, and
for a skirmish only : but the Maid would have
had it thorough, though her Inward Counsellors
had given her no call, nor advised nor forbidden.

She went on, therefore, under the rain of
arrows across the outer dry ditch, and over the
rampart, calling on all to follow, till she came
to the moat outside the towers and works of the
Gate (where now stands the Hotel of Normandy
in the Rue de l'Echelle) and there she tried the
depth of the water with her lance. But as she
so plumbed it, shouting for fascines, a cross-
bow shaft struck her through the armour of

the thigh and she went down, and lying there wounded she still urged on her men ; but the light was failing and the hopeless assault had failed. Thence as darkness gathered Alençon bore her away, for all her praying to remain there and her calling for one more blow.

In the days that followed, Charles of Valois wrote to all his cities saying that he now had peace with his good cousin of Burgundy and so could and would come back and " pursue what is left to me to conquer, the full recovery of my heritage." And having so written, his advisers, the men of policy and plot, dupes and entangled, broke off the war, and went back southward to the Loire again in retreat from that campaign which had held promise of such great things. But the Maid put off her white armour and laid it on the Altar of Our Lady in St. Denis minster, and being healed of her wound rode back southward sadly to the Loire with the King.

All that Autumn and through the Winter time, they lay in the country south of Loire, with arms but rarely sounding, and Joan was with them, taken to this Castle and to that, praised indeed and flattered, but having about her such looks as she could understand.

For now they said to themselves that she had outlived her brief effect, and that she could not understand the policy they had achieved, and that her simplicity and simple strokes of arms might ruin all.

So they would give her fine clothes and great horses and make her of their company in the weariness of the great, but she herself, her soul within, was unused and left aside. If they used her at all, it was to keep her from greater things, and to employ her hands lest her spirit should rebel. They let her carry the town of St. Pierre for such pastime, and fail once more (for she failed) at La Charité far south and east,

and of no service to the Cause. Nor to either place did her Voices send her, but they of the Court, who were blind to the things beyond this world.

Her family was ennobled, with a coat given it and a blazon, two lilies on a field azure and a sword with a crown. She herself cared nothing for such things, but she begged that her village of Domrémy and Greux its neighbour might be freed of taxes for ever : a privilege as yet unknown. So they stood free, until, in an evil day, after four hundred years, some officer of the treasury, contemptuous of such antiquities, ended them ; and soon after the Crown fell for ever.

But Joan awaited the Spring, and from Sully, the home of the false Trémoille, where the King lay, she left him without warning or farewell, determined upon war. It was in the later days of March, and Easter and the end of the

truce with Burgundy were near at hand. She
rode northward with but two lances or three, a
company of less than a score, making for Lagny
in the Paris part where some still made good
war against the English. And in Easter week,
which was the third week of April in that year,
fourteen hundred and thirty, with the Spring
about her, she stood on the ramparts of Melun,
and once more she was aware of the great light,
and her blessed Saints Catherine and Margaret
were before her speaking in their sweet voices a
new thing : for this is what they said :

" Before Midsummer Day you will be taken
captive, for so it is decreed. But do not fear
nor travail, but take all well, for God will be
your aid."

Thenceforward almost daily did she hear this
told. And she prayed that in the hour of her
capture she might die and be spared, of grace,
long prison. But they told her that prison she

must bear, and when she asked the hour of this fate, they were silent. From that day onward she had these things in her heart, yet did she ride and ride, and on to Compiègne.

Now as for Compiègne—with which the King had thought to bribe Burgundy, but the men of Compiègne would have none of it—he had given it to La Trémoille, who governed him, to take the revenue of it as its lord; but La Trémoille appointed for Captain over the King's forces there, one William of Flavy, brigandish but brave, and determined not to yield; a good holder of walls. And the reason Burgundy had coveted Compiègne was this, that it was the bulwark of Paris.

For until the Maid had freed Orleans or crowned the King at Rheims and got the many towns of the North, all about Paris was under the Plantagenets and their Burgundian allies, and Bedford was secure in the holding of his

capital for the boy his nephew, Henry, King of England, and Burgundy could come in and out at will and keep his garrison there well provisioned and secure. But after so many towns round about Paris had fallen to the Valois, the great city was hampered, and chiefly through Compiègne. For Compiègne lay right on the river Oise and the road along its banks, which road and river were the highways from Picardy and the Lowlands, Burgundy's own country, to Paris by water and by land, for men marching and for boat-loads and munitions of every kind.

Therefore when the truce was ended, with Easter Day, which fell on the sixteenth of April of that year fourteen hundred and thirty, Burgundy made great preparation to take Compiègne. And therefore also did Joan ride thither to succour it. And during the first week of May and the second she went up and down through the countrysides to seize bridges

and holds and to prevent the siege ; for now upon Compiègne, as once on Orleans, hung the Cause.

But in the matter of Compiègne her Voices gave her no bidding.

Now when it was found that the forces of Burgundy had worked so hard and taken bridges and had so ravaged the countryside that there was no sustenance left for her little army, it was disbanded ; but she herself would enter Compiègne with a small company and by her name and presence give it heart, and at sunrise upon Tuesday the twenty-third of May she rode in.

The city lay, as does Orleans, hard on the river bank, but looking northward ; and it was much of a size with Orleans. Also its wall ran right along the riverside, and in the midst of it was a gate, called the Water Gate, with ditch and drawbridge and portcullis, leading to a long bridge going northward across the river Oise ;

and on the farther northern shore was a bridge-head fortified, and thence, onwards, a causeway of hard road going over the water-meadows towards the higher land beyond : and on this higher land lay Burgundy's men, threatening the town.

When it was already evening of that day, but the sun still high, the Maid rode out with them of Compiègne and her own company, by the Water Gate and over the bridge and along the causeway to beat up the Burgundian quarters and harry them, that she might confuse their beginning of work against the town. But in that same hour they were reinforced by new companies with certain of the English also, and she fell back with her command by the cause-way towards the bridge, she herself in the rear guard, holding the press of the foe and showing clear in her broidered coat above her armour.

But the Burgundian force swelled and grew

so strong that it swamped this retiring column till they fled, with the enemy all intermixed among them, over the bridge to the Water Gate beyond. And as they flew in pell-mell, Flavy, to keep out the shouting mass of the foemen pursuing, drew up the drawbridge and lowered the portcullis. But away beyond the bridge on the far water-meadows Joan, her company and her Knight D'Aulnon, and Peter her brother, and the rest, were surrounded as they fought desperately to keep back the tide. And the archer of a Captain who served that one-eyed Lord, John of Luxemburg (Burgundy's right-hand man), caught her by the coat and dragged her from the horse and took her captive. So the day ended. And Compiègne still held.

.   .   .   .   .

When it was known that the Maid was prisoner, great rumour rose and ran through all the North. Charles of Valois raged, this once

in his life, and promised vengeance. But soon his courtiers lowered his tone. Burgundy himself triumphed, and for Bedford and the English it seemed an end. The University of Paris exulted, being fierce against the Valois, but most of them all did that Bishop Peter Cauchon exult whom the University held for a headman and protector, and whom, by the Maid, the Valois had driven from his Bishopric of Beauvais in the summer past, when the cities were returning to their King. He was a man full of strong evil and, more than any other man, would he labour to serve whomsoever might oppose the Blood Royal : Burgundy or Bedford or another.

He went up and down clamouring for the custody of the Maid, and the University called for her to be tried in Paris, for Heresy, for Witchcraft, for Idolatry.

But by the laws of war she was Luxemburg's

prize, he being overlord of them that took her.
So first he had her brought, after some two
weeks or three in other places, to his strong
castle of Beaurevoir near to Le Catelet, and
there she was guarded ; but not with harshness,
for Luxemburg's ladies, his aunt and wife, were
kind to her. And all the while Cauchon
travelled hither and thither, well paid by
Bedford, into Flanders, to before Compiègne
to see Burgundy, to Beaurevoir itself, demanding
the Maid. And he had mission to plead that
the English King might claim Joan of right as
his prisoner, being overlord, and it being against
the English that she had used her witchcraft.
But his pleading would have availed nothing had
he not also offered gold. For Bedford had
raised a great tax in Normandy, and out of this
had set aside twenty thousand pounds wherewith to buy the Maid. And this Cauchon
still offered, until in October, before Martin-

mas, the bargain was struck and Luxemburg agreed that Joan should be given up and sold against that money.

But she heard of it, there in the tower of Beaurevoir, and she so hated falling into the hands of the English and feared for the fate of Compiègne, that she would escape by cloths tied together, from the high tower, though St. Catharine had daily forbidden it and had told her that by Martinmas Compiègne would be freed. Never before nor after did she disobey. She fell and lay without sense on the ground below, till they brought her back to her captivity. And now she had been sold, and from thence, to the grief of Luxemburg's ladies, she was borne away by them that had bought her, and under an English guard.

They took her by Drugy to the sea-towns, by Crotoy and across the shallow Bay to St. Valéry, through the arch where is now the

deserted road, to Eu, to Dieppe, and thence by Arques and Longueville to Rouen, where she was to be tried for witchcraft. And there they closely prisoned her, at the end of the year, in the castle of the town, chained by the neck and both hands and both feet in a narrow dungeon, and guarded by five common grooms of Warwick's garrison. These took it in turns, three to stand by and sleep in that narrow den, two to watch without; and they mocked her and jeered, and with insults intolerable made her life hellish thence onward till she died. And in dread of them and their lechery she kept her man's clothes and would not take a woman's.

Then, by writ of the third of January, the trial was ordered to be held, ecclesiastical; it was for heresy and witchcraft and blasphemy that she was to be tried: for of the Devil was her power, and Charles of Valois must be put in league with foul things, the enemy of man-

kind, and cloaked in shame. And she herself must carry infamy for ever in vengeance for the defeats of the English which she had guided. Now as she was to be tried by a Church Court, she should have been in the Church prison, and with only woman about her. But Cauchon who ordered all, broke that sacred law, for Bedford had sent word that even if she were acquitted in her trial before the Priests she must not be let free, but given back to the Rouen garrison and Warwick its commander.

For five months the case proceeded, Cauchon and the Vice-Inquisitor Le Maitre being the judges, and summoning to their court more than forty Bishops and Abbots and Doctors of Church Law for assessors. But Le Maitre would have withdrawn, till under threat he yielded ; and although the assessors were carefully chosen for the work, yet even among them some few seemed not subservient ; and being threatened

also, they fled. First that Court gathered testimony during some weeks, questioning her, and sending for matter to Domrémy itself and to all places where she had been and where their messengers might have access, putting together all that she had done, and the marvels to show that they were done by witchcraft, and her assurance in her Brethren of Paradise that they might make it out Pride and a defiance of God.

Then they held public session in the Castle Chapel, forty-two, with Cauchon presiding, and questioned her with pitfall and trap. But she answered steadily day by day, still clear for all her abominable nights and days. For they still chained her all one month and another and another in that dungeon, with such foul warders, until her soul was drowned in agony and numbed ; nor had she any woman about her nor any friend, nor any surcease from abominations of word and deed in the half-day of that gloom,

K

and in the dreadful nights.   But still she stood
fast.

Also when they took her out, one day, and
another, to make question, she still spoke high,
warning Cauchon what peril he ran for his
soul.   She told the story of her Voices and her
Visions, simple and strong, in answer to their
examinations, and on one famous day in March
she gave a sign once more, saying :

"Within seven years the English will lose a
greater prize than Orleans, and then all France."
And indeed in the sixth year Paris fell and in
the eight the last battle was fought at Formigny.

And one more sign she gave, which she herself
did not comprehend ; for she told how her
Voices had bidden her not heed her sufferings,
for thence should she come to the Kingdom of
Paradise, and within three months she would
be free.   Now within three months lacking one
day from the hour in which she spoke thus, she

was indeed set free from this accursed world. But because her Voices had spoken of freedom, she thought they had promised rescue, and she thought it would come perhaps by a victory or in a tumult.

She gave also another sign. For she said that soon by a Great Arrangement all the Kingdom should act together, and this also came true. For a last and firm treaty between Burgundy and the King was signed whereby within three years the English power was extinguished.

On one thing only she would not speak, for she held herself bound to shield the honour of her King. It was the King's secret she would not give them: that prayer in which he had doubted the Blood Royal. But, being pressed beyond bearing, she gave them a parable and told them that the secret was the coming of an Angel, a messenger from Heaven to Chinon, bearing him a crown, which was the sign.

" And that crown he has still." But it was a figure only. By that Messenger Joan meant herself, and the crown was the crown of the Realm wherewith Charles of Valois, her Dauphin, had been crowned at Rheims.

They did not torture her with racks and screws ; though they debated on it. They voted other. But they brought her to the edges of endurance, till she fell into sickness ; when Warwick summoned the doctor to warn him that she must not die by nature. And still they wore her down.

Then at last, in Whitweek, she having lain in that foul dungeon four months, and it being one year since her capture (for it was Wednesday the twenty-third of May, and evening), Peter Maurice, a priest who had served at the trial, came and spoke to her with reason, and exhorted her in loyalty to God, and in soldierly honour to accept authority and to submit. Also, perhaps

he did not lie in his soul but thought that she was indeed deluded, and desired out of pity to save her from the fire. And all that dreadful night she had these things to think upon, awaiting the morrow.

And on that morrow, Thursday the twenty-fourth of May, they prepared that public ceremony, which in such trials ecclesiastical was called " the Abjuration." For if the arraigned would recant, their lives were spared, and all must have opportunity so to save themselves from the fire. It was law and practice unbroken, and therefore it was done ; although to some of her captors it was grievous, lest she should yield and they lose her. But Cauchon knew well his part and how, by some forced confession of witchcraft from her, she and her King could first be made infamous, and how later, by a further hell, she could be goaded to the fire none the less ; and thus both his ends

would be fulfilled—to destroy her name and to take bodily vengeance.

There is in this town of Rouen a great church called St. Ouen, and beside it was a cemetery, a wide field, for it was to the east on the outer part of the town ; and here was a hustings put up to which Joan should be led, that she might be seen by all the multitude. And while Joan was seated upon this platform with a desk before her, there was read out to her a long list and close of her errors and crimes of heresy and witchcraft, that having heard it, she might say whether she would abjure them or no. But she could make nothing of it all.

Then one Erard, the official for that task, read to her a short paper of eight lines, no longer than a Pater Noster, wherein—as is supposed—she was made only in general words to confess wrong doing and to abjure it ; and they promised by words (but were careful not

to have it in writing) that if she would sign and wear woman's clothes in proof of repentance, they would take her from the abomination of her prison and those vile men and take off the chains and put her, as had been her right from the first, into the Prison of the Bishop, where she should be tended by women only, as the law of the Church requires. And Joan put her sign to this paper, having, as she did so, upon her face a smile, the meaning of which we cannot know.

But when the multitude saw that she had signed, some, who pitied her, were glad that she had escaped the fire, and others, very few, who thought her holy, grieved ; but the many, and especially the English lords and their soldiers, were angry to madness, thinking she had escaped them. And stones were thrown, and there was a tumult, and Joan was led away. But as for Cauchon, he broke his word and had them take her, not to the Church prison,

unchained, with women to tend her, but to the Castle dungeon, chained, and to the company of those grooms through horror of whom she had signed. And they gave her woman's clothes, and she wore them : being now at the mercy of those grooms.

And certain priests desiring further to question her came on the next day to the Castle Court, but there the soldiers of Warwick cursed them for false Armagnacs that had saved the Witch from the fire : they not knowing how in those same days Cauchon himself had said to the lords who reproached him : " We shall catch her yet ! "

Now on the Sunday morning she would rise, and she said to those grooms : " Loose my chains, for I have need to rise." Then one of them took away her woman's dress that lay on the bed and brought, in a bag, the man's dress she had worn before her Abjuration ; and he

pulled it out of the bag and laid it on the bed before her. Then she would not rise, seeing that she only had this to wear; for she said: "It is forbidden me." But when it was already midday she could hold out no longer, and she put on her man's dress as before.

And when it was known the next day that she was so dressed, eight of her judges came and asked her why she had again taken on men's clothes; and they told her that this was Relapse. But she said that being among such men she was compelled, and she told with disfigured face and bitter tears the outrages attempted. And she upbraided her judges for their breach of faith. On the next day again, being Tuesday, Cauchon gathered his tribe about him and they condemned her for a Renegade Relapsed, to be handed over early upon the morrow to the Secular Arm and the Fire.

Now when the morning had come, being Wednesday the thirtieth day of May in the year of Our Lord fourteen hundred and thirty-one, the two Dominicans who had been with her during the trial came to tell her that she must die, and by what death. And on hearing this she fell into a violent sobbing and moaning, writhing and tearing at her hair and crying out that rather had she died seven times by the axe than that her pure and uncorrupted body should be burned.

Then Peter Cauchon, that evil Bishop, came into the dungeon and she said to him: "Bishop, it is by you that I die! Had you put me in the Church's prison with women to guard me as was of right, this would not have been. I summon you before God the great Judge."

They asked her also whether she did not now believe her Voices false, since she had found no deliverance. But whether in bitterness she

murmured yes, or whether she answered with a guarded word, we cannot tell : for the testimony is confused. It was the Hour of Evil and the Powers of Darkness were abroad. But this we know : that she had heard her Saints reproaching her for that lapse of hers when she had signed, and that, on their reproaches, she repented.

Whatever her answer, they relented in the matter of the Communion, which she had been so long denied. The Mass, which she had longed for through all that dereliction, she might not hear ; but she received the Body of the Lord.

Then they put on her a long white dress and set her in the tumbril with the Dominican who was to be with her till the end. And as she went up into the tumbril she asked of Peter Maurice who stood by :

"Master Maurice, where shall I be to-night ?"

Who answered : " Have you no trust in God ? "

And she said : " Yes. This day shall I be in Paradise."

Now they had set a guard about her of two hundred men with staves and pikes who went before her through a press of people in the streets on either side, and they slowly thrusting through, went down with her towards the market-square ; and as she went and over-looked the town she said : " Ah ! Rouen, Rouen, do I die here in you, and are you to be my last habitation ? "

And when they had come into the market-square there was a great concourse of many thousands awaiting them, and in the midst (but somewhat to the western side) was a heap of mortar very high, hardened to stone, and a tall stake standing in it, and the faggots piled around it. These, after one deputed had

preached at her, she mounted without faltering, and was chained to the stake. But being there, above the people, and seen by all, she forgave her enemies and begged each priest in that multitude to say one mass for her soul.

Then she asked for a Cross, and an English soldier bound two sticks together and held it up for her to take, which she kissed and put into the bosom of her white robe. She asked also for a Crucifix from the Church at hand, and this was found and given her. And when she had held this up before her and kissed it also fervently while the English lords clamoured at the delay, the torch was set to the faggots, and in the midst of the smoke they heard her proclaiming firmly that indeed her Mission was of God, and they heard her praying to the Saints ; till, in a very little while, a loud voice came from the midst of the burning, the Holy Name JESUS, called so loudly that every man

heard it to the very ends of the Square. And
after that there was silence, and no sound but
the crackling of the fire.

Order was given for the embers to be pulled
apart so that all might see she was dead. But
lest her relics should be worshipped, men were
bidden bear her ashes to the river Seine which
ran near by. So they threw into the river the
ashes of that Maiden, and her heart, which the
fire had not consumed.

PRINTED BY WYMAN AND SONS, LTD.,
LONDON, FAKENHAM AND READING
F. 30. 830